Pebble Plus

BIG

BIG PETS

by Catherine Ipcizade

Consulting Editor: Gail Saunders-Smith, PhD

Consultant: Jennifer Zablotny, DVM
Member, American Veterinary Medical Association

CAPSTONE PRESS
a capstone imprint

Pebble Plus is published by Capstone Press,
151 Good Counsel Drive, P.O. Box 669, Mankato, Minnesota 56002.
www.capstonepress.com

Printed in the United States of America in North Mankato, Minnesota

092009
005618CGS10

Books published by Capstone Press are manufactured with paper containing at least 10 percent post-consumer waste.

Library of Congress Cataloging-in-Publication Data
Ipcizade, Catherine.
Big pets / by Catherine Ipcizade.
p. cm. — (Pebble plus. Big)
Includes bibliographical references and index.
Summary: "Simple text and photographs describe big pets" — Provided by publisher.
ISBN 978-1-4296-3997-2 (library binding)
1. Pets — Miscellanea — Juvenile literature. 2. Pets — Size — Juvenile literature. I. Title. II. Series.
SF416.I63 2010
636.088'7 — dc22 2009026267

Editorial credits
Erika L. Shores, editor; Ted Williams, designer; Wanda Winch, media researcher; Eric Manske, production specialist

Photo credits
Capstone Studio/Karon Dubke, all

Note to Parents and Teachers

The Big set supports national science standards related to life science. This book describes and illustrates big pets. The images support early readers in understanding the text. The repetition of words and phrases helps early readers learn new words. This book also introduces early readers to subject-specific vocabulary words, which are defined in the Glossary section. Early readers may need assistance to read some words and to use the Table of Contents, Glossary, Read More, Internet Sites, and Index sections of the book.

Table of Contents

Big

Big pets need room to play and plenty of food to eat. Caring for big pets can be tons of fun.

Giant breeds of rabbits weigh 12 pounds (5 kilograms) or more.

Koi start out as small fish.
They grow quickly.
Big backyard ponds give them room to grow.

Size:
up to 36 inches
(91 centimeters) long

Macaws are noisy pets. They open big beaks to squawk. Owners can teach these birds to say words.

Size:
up to 36 inches (91 centimeters) long from head to tail

Bigger

Maine Coons are the biggest cat breed. Owners enjoy caring for these playful pets.

Size:
up to 20 pounds
(9 kilograms)

Green iguanas are long reptiles. These pets live in big cages.

Size:

up to 6.5 feet (2 meters) long from head to tail

Potbellied pigs are smart. Owners teach these big pets to sit for treats.

Size:
up to 200 pounds
(91 kilograms)

Biggest

Mastiffs are the biggest breed of dog. Mastiffs weigh up to 230 pounds (104 kilograms).

Size:

34 inches (86 centimeters) tall at shoulder

Reptile experts own pet boa constrictors. These big snakes can live up to 35 years.

Size:
up to 14 feet
(4.3 meters) long

Symposium

Owning a horse is a big job.
Horses need exercise
and brushing every day.
Owners enjoy time
with their loyal pets.

Size:

up to 68 inches (172 centimeters) tall from ground to top of shoulder

Glossary

beak — the hard, pointed part of a bird's mouth

breed — a certain kind of animal within an animal group

cage — a container in which an animal is kept

exercise — to be active

expert — someone who knows a great deal about a subject

loyal — faithful to a person

reptile — a cold-blooded animal with a backbone

Read More

Pipe, Jim. *Pets.* Read and Play. North Mankato, Minn.: Stargazer Books, 2008.

Salzmann, Mary Elizabeth. *Brilliant Birds.* Perfect Pets. Edina, Minn.: Abdo, 2007.

Schaefer, Lola M. *Family Pets.* Families. Mankato, Minn.: Capstone Press, 2008.

Internet Sites

FactHound offers a safe, fun way to find Internet sites related to this book. All of the sites on FactHound have been researched by our staff.

Here's all you do:

Visit *www.facthound.com*

FactHound will fetch the best sites for you!

Index

Word Count: 145
Grade: 1
Early-Intervention Level: 14